A BUSINESS APPROACH TO MELON FARMING

I0430028

Complete Entrepreneurial Step By Step Guide To Melon Garden From Scratch

ZHURI HART

DISCLAIMER

This book is intended to provide general information and insights on adopting a business approach to farming. The content within is based on the author's knowledge and experiences up to the date of publication. It is essential to recognize that the field of agriculture is dynamic, influenced by various factors such as market conditions, climate, and regulatory changes.

Readers are advised to conduct thorough research, seek professional advice, and consider their unique circumstances before implementing any strategies or practices discussed in this book. The author and publisher disclaim any responsibility for the accuracy, completeness, or suitability of the information provided. The book is not a substitute for professional advice, and the author and publisher shall not be liable for any damages or losses arising from the use or reliance on the information presented herein.

Individual results may vary, and success in farming enterprises is contingent upon numerous variables. The author encourages readers to consult with relevant experts, agricultural extension services, and legal or financial professionals to tailor strategies to their specific needs and local conditions.

This book is not intended to be a comprehensive guide to all aspects of farming, and readers should exercise their judgment and discretion in applying the principles discussed. The author and publisher do not endorse any specific products, services, or companies mentioned in this book unless explicitly stated.

By reading this book, the reader acknowledges and accepts the inherent uncertainties in agricultural endeavors and agrees to use the information at their own risk.

TABLE OF CONTENTS

ABOUT THE BOOK

"A Business Approach to Melon Farming," a book written for entrepreneurs wishing to enter this agricultural industry, explores the complex and sometimes disregarded world of melon farming. The book's introduction lays out the important history of melon growing and highlights its importance to the commercial world. The goals outlined highlight the useful results that readers might anticipate and offer a path for gaining the necessary information and abilities.

The book goes over popular types and their varietal features to help readers comprehend melon varieties. This information serves as the basis for further decision-making procedures, which are discussed in the market research and analysis section. The book skillfully walks readers through the process of determining target markets, evaluating market demand, analyzing competitors, and keeping abreast of market trends—all crucial components of any prosperous agricultural business.

Subsequently, the book delves into the topic of melon farming business planning. It guides creating an extensive company plan, establishing realistic targets and benchmarks, and anticipating financial concerns. Risk management techniques give a practical touch by addressing the inherent uncertainties in agricultural endeavors.

The specifics of setting up ideal circumstances for melon growing are covered in detail in the chapters on on-site preparation and selection. This part presents a comprehensive picture that is essential for successful farming operations, covering everything from soil requirements and climate concerns to land preparation procedures and necessary infrastructure.

The book goes on to provide advice on managing melon crops, including how to plant, how to water, how to fertilize, and how to handle pests and diseases. The focus on post-harvest management and harvesting guarantees a thorough comprehension of the melon growing lifecycle.

In the highly competitive market, quality standards and certification are critical. The book tackles these issues by explaining how to fulfill quality requirements, delving into organic melon cultivation, and outlining the certification procedures. This information is a great help to farmers who want to differentiate their goods in the marketplace.

The book carefully negotiates financial management, legal issues, and marketing tactics. Each component is carefully addressed, offering a comprehensive view of running a profitable melon farming business. From branding and packaging to creating a marketing plan, budgeting, cost analysis, pricing strategies, and compliance with legal and regulatory standards, every detail is taken care of.

"A Business Approach to Melon Farming" proves to be a priceless tool for business owners looking to start a melon farming operation.

CHAPTER ONE

MELON FARMING INTRODUCTION

MELON FARMING'S SIGNIFICANCE TO BUSINESS

Melon growing is an important economic and agricultural endeavor that can be quite profitable for both farmers and businesses. In addition to offering consumers an important source of nutrition, melons offer a variety of economic prospects for individuals working in the agriculture industry. Melons are an important product in the market, contributing to the agricultural and economic landscapes due to their widespread popularity and simple variety.

It is impossible to overestimate the significance of melon cultivation in the corporate world. Melons are prized for many uses in the food business in addition to their delicious flavor and high nutritional value. Melon has been a culinary mainstay, used in everything from fresh food to drinks, salads, and desserts. Because of its adaptability, melon farming is a profitable enterprise that allows growers to serve a wide range of customers and penetrate different market niches.

RECOGNIZING DIFFERENT MELON TYPES

It's essential to comprehend the wide range of melon types for effective marketing and farming. Melons are available in a range of sizes, shapes, and flavors, and each type has its special qualities.

Farmers and business owners need to become knowledgeable about the wide variety of melon options available so they can decide what to cultivate depending on their personal preferences, market demand, and environment. A vital component of optimizing the potential for a profitable and long-lasting melon-growing enterprise is this understanding.

COMMON MELONS

Common varieties of melons highlight the variety and depth of this fruit group even more. Melons come in a variety of flavors and textures, from the popularly consumed watermelon with its juicy, sweet flesh to cantaloupes with its fragrant, orange-hued core. Among the other well-known melon types, Honeydew, Crenshaw, and Casaba each provide unique attributes to the market. To provide customers with a diverse and enticing choice, growers and business owners must investigate the distinctive qualities of these popular melon varieties.

VARIETAL FEATURES

A key factor in determining the success of melon growing endeavors is variability's. Taste, texture, scent, and shelf life are a few examples of factors that affect customer demand and market preferences. To customize their cultivation tactics and produce melons that not only match consumer expectations but also stand out in the competitive market, farmers must carefully evaluate these varietal traits. This knowledge of varietal subtleties helps farmers choose crops wisely, which in turn affects the productivity and profitability of their melon farming operations.

SELECTING THE BEST MELON FOR YOUR ENTERPRISE

Selecting the ideal melon for a company requires a calculated strategy that considers several variables. When choosing which melon types to cultivate, farmers and business owners need to take into account consumer preferences, market trends, and local climate conditions. The logistical considerations of storage and transportation are also quite important when making decisions. Making an informed decision guarantees that the melons produced meet market demands, which leads to a more lucrative and sustainable business strategy. In summary, the significance of melon farming for business goes beyond the production of a well-liked fruit; rather, it represents a dynamic and strategic endeavor that, to succeed in the always-changing agricultural landscape, demands close attention to varietal characteristics and market dynamics.

CHAPTER TWO

ANALYSIS AND RESEARCH ON THE MARKET

EVALUATING DEMAND IN THE MARKET

One of the most important components of any thorough market research plan is evaluating consumer demand. It entails figuring out how much demand there is in a certain market for a specific good or service. Analyzing variables including consumer preferences, purchase patterns, and economic developments is frequently a part of this process.

Companies can use a range of techniques, including focus groups, surveys, and data analytics, to precisely determine market demand.

Businesses can better fulfill the demands and expectations of their target audience and become more competitive in the market by customizing their services based on a thorough assessment of market demand.

DETERMINING THE TARGET MARKET

Developing an effective marketing strategy starts with identifying your target audience. This is identifying the traits, actions, and tastes of the perfect client for a good or service. Businesses can efficiently direct their marketing efforts by developing comprehensive client profiles using behavioral, psychographic, and demographic data. Businesses may adjust their messaging, distribution methods, and product features to appeal to the target market by knowing the requirements and driving forces of their target market. This customer-focused strategy raises general consumer happiness and loyalty in addition to increasing the effectiveness of marketing campaigns.

ANALYSIS OF COMPETITORS

An essential part of market research is competition analysis, which entails assessing the advantages and disadvantages of both present and potential rivals. Businesses can recognize market possibilities and risks by comprehending the competitive landscape. This research includes looking at the goods, prices, promotions, and general market positioning of rival companies. Companies can use SWOT analysis (Strengths, Weaknesses, Opportunities, Threats) techniques to learn more about their advantages and disadvantages over rivals. In-depth competitor analysis is helpful not just in developing winning marketing plans but also in presenting goods and services in a way that makes them stand out in the marketplace.

OPPORTUNITIES & MARKET TRENDS

Businesses looking to develop steadily must keep an eye on market trends and spot possibilities. Market trends include modifications to consumer inclinations, advances in technology, and adjustments to the regulatory landscape. Businesses can adjust their tactics to fit the changing market landscape by keeping up with these changes. Finding unmet demands or new market gaps that a business can fill is part of the opportunity identification process.

By taking a proactive stance, companies can use unexplored markets or tailor their products to suit evolving customer needs. Businesses can get a strategic advantage by routinely assessing market trends and spotting possibilities. This helps them remain ahead of the competition and make wise decisions that will lead to long-term success.

CHAPTER THREE

MELON FARMING BUSINESS PLANNING

MAKING A BUSINESS STRATEGY

A thorough business plan must be created if melon farming is to be successful. This document, which outlines the objectives, tactics, and specifics of the business's operations, acts as a roadmap. An extensive study of the melon industry that identifies the main trends, rivals, and target clientele should be the first step in any company plan. It should clearly define the goals and objectives of the melon farming company, giving it a feeling of direction and purpose.

The business plan should include an organizational structure that delineates critical roles and duties, in addition to a market study. The production process, including how melons will be grown, harvested, and distributed to markets, should also be covered in this part. A strong business plan not only draws in possible investors but also functions as a useful guide for the management group, assisting them in decision-making and helping them adjust to shifting market conditions.

CREATING OBJECTIVES AND BENCHMARKS

The foundation of any successful melon-growing enterprise is the establishment of precise and quantifiable objectives. Both short- and long-term objectives, including things like production targets, market share, and financial performance, should be included in goals. Milestones serve as roadblocks that the company may use to monitor its development and make necessary corrections.

A melon farming enterprise may aim to maximize operational efficiency, increase market reach, or increase yield per acre. It is vital to guarantee that these objectives are time-bound, meaningful, quantifiable, achievable, and specific (SMART). Maintaining the business's agility and responsiveness to market changes requires regular reviews and updates of goals and milestones.

BUDGETARY ESTIMATES

A melon farming business plan must include accurate financial predictions since they offer a reasonable estimate of earnings, costs, and profitability. A thorough analysis of the start-up costs, continuing operating costs, and revenue streams should be included in this section.

Additionally, it might estimate balance sheets, profit and loss statements, and cash flow for several years.

By illustrating the possible return on investment, financial projections help to secure money from lenders or investors. When making financial forecasts, it is crucial to take into account factors including market demand, seasonal swings, and prospective dangers.

By periodically reviewing and revising these estimates, the company can adjust to evolving conditions and make well-informed financial choices.

TECHNIQUES FOR RISK MANAGEMENT

Like any agricultural endeavor, melons are susceptible to several dangers, such as unfavorable weather, pests, and unstable markets. Creating efficient risk management plans is essential to reducing any risks and guaranteeing the company's long-term viability. This entails determining the main risks, estimating the possible consequences, and putting policies in place to reduce or transfer these risks.

A melon farming business may choose to diversify its crops, put pest control measures in place, and purchase insurance as risk management tactics. Regular risk monitoring and evaluation are crucial, and plans should be adjusted as necessary to meet new obstacles. Including resilience in the business plan improves the overall stability of the melon farming industry by reducing the impact of unanticipated events.

CHAPTER FOUR

CHOOSING AND SETTING UP THE SITE

SOIL CONDITIONS

Any project's preparation and site selection are critical phases, and the decision-making process is influenced by several variables. The chosen site's requirements for soil are one of the primary factors. The success of a variety of endeavors, including construction and agriculture, is directly impacted by the kind and quality of soil. When choosing a site, it is crucial to carefully consider the fertility, drainage, and composition of the soil. A thorough soil analysis can provide crucial details regarding pH balance, nutrient levels, and potential problems, enabling stakeholders to decide on the best use of the land.

CLIMATE-RELATED ISSUES

The effectiveness and sustainability of a project can be greatly impacted by the local weather, so climate considerations are crucial when choosing a site. Evaluating variables such as seasonal fluctuations, precipitation levels, and temperature ranges is necessary to comprehend the climatic conditions. Selecting a location with a climate that is appropriate for the planned crops is important for agriculture, but for other enterprises, factors like temperature swings and extreme weather events become critical. To guarantee long-term profitability and resilience, the objective is to match the project's requirements with the site's climate.

TECHNIQUES FOR LAND PREPARATION

Techniques for preparing the land are crucial to converting the chosen location into a useful area that satisfies project specifications. These methods entail several procedures meant to maximize the land for the desired use. Common land preparation techniques include removing vegetation, leveling uneven terrain, and treating soil compaction. Modern equipment, such as excavators and bulldozers, makes it easier to prepare land effectively and guarantees a solid base for building or farming. Effective land preparation lowers the possibility of unforeseen issues and creates the foundation for a project's best possible performance.

FACILITIES AND GEAR

Equipment and infrastructure are essential to the preparation and selection of a location. The accessibility of essential infrastructure, like utilities, roads, and water supplies, has a direct impact on a project's viability and economy of scale. Having access to transportation networks is essential for personnel and products to be moved. Furthermore, the availability of dependable utilities guarantees a steady and ongoing supply of necessary resources. Equally important is choosing the right tools for land preparation. In addition to speeding up the process, modern machinery improves precision and reduces environmental effects. Sufficient funding for equipment and infrastructure has a major role in the project's overall viability.

The procedures of site selection and preparation are complex and call for a thorough evaluation of a variety of factors, including the availability of infrastructure and equipment, soil requirements, climate, and land preparation methods. By taking a comprehensive approach to these variables, one can make sure that the site is ideal for the project's goals and provide the groundwork for a successful, long-lasting outcome.

CHAPTER FIVE

MELON CROP MANAGEMENT

PLANTING METHODS

Successful melon crop management depends on using effective planting methods. Farmers need to think about things like climate, soil type, and variety choices. Melons grow best on soil that has enough drainage and airflow. To guarantee sufficient sunlight penetration and ventilation, plants must be spaced appropriately, which lowers the risk of illness. Farmers frequently employ direct seeding or transplanting techniques, taking into account the unique needs of the melon variety as well as the temperature of the area. Planting melons at the right time and depth will ensure a fruitful and healthy harvest.

IRRIGATION SYSTEMS

Growing melon crops requires effective water management. Throughout their growth phases, melons need regular and adequate water, with a focus on preventing water stress. For melon crops, drip irrigation systems are frequently used because they offer precise control over water distribution, minimize waste, and lower the danger of foliar diseases. For optimal water use efficiency and high-quality melon production, effective irrigation scheduling based on crop requirements and environmental factors is essential.

FERTILIZATION TECHNIQUES

To meet the dietary requirements of the plants, balanced fertilization is essential to the management of melon crops. To ascertain nutrient levels and direct fertilizer delivery, soil testing is frequently carried out. To encourage fruit growth, melons usually benefit from a fertilizer blend with a greater potassium ratio. Micronutrients, phosphorus, and nitrogen are also necessary for the general health of plants. Fertilizer choices for farmers might vary depending on personal preferences and environmental factors.

Maintaining healthy melon plants requires regular fertilization practice adjustments and monitoring.

CONTROL OF PESTS AND DISEASES

Good control of pests and diseases is essential to the proper maintenance of melon crops. To reduce the amount of chemical pesticides used, integrated pest management (IPM) techniques are frequently used. One of the main components of Integrated Pest Management (IPM) is the use of natural predators, resistant melon varieties, and early detection of pests and diseases. Aphids, mites, and whiteflies are common pests of melons, and diseases like bacterial wilt and powdery mildew can be serious hazards.

HARVESTING AND POST-HARVEST HANDLING

For optimal flavor, texture, and overall quality, melons must be harvested at the proper stage of maturity. Certain melon types have distinct ripeness markers, like firmness, color, and aroma. Hand harvesting ensures that the fruit is damaged as little as possible. To preserve quality, post-harvest management calls for cautious storage and transportation. Melon shelf life can be increased with proper cooling and humidity control. Fruit should be packaged to keep it safe from outside pollutants and physical harm. For the harvested melons to remain fresh and retain their market value, they must be transported from the farm to the market quickly and effectively.

CHAPTER SIX

CERTIFICATION THAT COMPLIES WITH QUALITY STANDARDS

A vital component of guaranteeing the general excellence and dependability of goods or services is meeting quality standards. Standards of quality act as benchmarks, defining acceptable performance, safety, and other parameters. Following these guidelines is important for a variety of businesses not only to comply with legal requirements but also to gain the trust of stakeholders and customers. To monitor and control processes and guarantee that goods and services continuously meet or surpass predetermined standards, businesses frequently implement strict quality management systems.

ORGANIC FARMING OF MELON

Organic melon growing is one particular industry where upholding quality standards are crucial. By avoiding the use of artificial pesticides, herbicides, and genetically modified organisms, organic farming emphasizes environmentally friendly and sustainable farming methods. Organic melon growers prioritize soil health, biodiversity, and ecological balance in their quest to produce high-quality fruits. Usually, relevant certifying bodies use certification procedures to verify compliance with organic farming requirements.

PROCEDURES FOR CERTIFICATION

Certification procedures are essential for verifying that quality requirements are being followed, especially when it comes to organic melon growing. Farmers' adherence to the recommended organic agricultural procedures is evaluated and confirmed by certifying authorities, which are frequently accredited organizations.

To make sure that the production techniques adhere to organic standards, these procedures entail documentation checks, on-site inspections, and other assessments. Obtaining certification offers concrete proof of a farmer's dedication to quality, sustainability, and customer standards.

The procedure of certification is complex when it comes to organic melon growing. Before applying for certification, farmers must adopt organic techniques for a predetermined amount of time. Using organic seeds, avoiding synthetic inputs, and implementing crop rotation techniques are a few examples of how to do this. Inspectors thoroughly assess a farmer's farming methods, soil management, pest control, and general adherence to organic principles when they receive an application for certification. Farmers that are successful in obtaining certification can mark their melons as "certified organic," giving customers confidence in the product's excellence and compliance with strict guidelines.

PROMOTING ORGANIC MELONS

One of the main strategies for marketing organic melons is to highlight their certification status. The accreditation is a reliable and easily identifiable mark of excellence and sustainability. Marketing ads highlight how organic melon cultivation is health-conscious and environmentally sustainable. Emphasizing the lack of artificial chemicals and the dedication to moral agricultural methods appeals to customers who value their health, the environment, and sustainable farming.

Melons that are certified organic frequently have a niche market among buyers who are looking for high-end, eco-friendly goods. Transparent labeling, certification emblems, and narratives that highlight the farmer's commitment to organic farming are examples of marketing tactics. By informing customers about the advantages of selecting certified organic melons, you may build a relationship between the farmer and the final customer as well as encourage brand loyalty.

CHAPTER SEVEN

ADVERTISING TECHNIQUES

PACKAGING AND BRANDING

A company's identity and customer perceptions are greatly shaped by its branding and packaging. Beyond only a logo, branding encompasses a company's complete character, principles, and commitments. A strong brand strategy builds a relationship with the intended audience and encourages loyalty and trust. A cohesive and memorable brand image is ensured by maintaining consistency in branding across a range of touch points, from commercials to consumer interactions.

FORMULATING A MARKETING STRATEGY

Contrarily, packaging serves as a potent marketing technique in addition to being a product's protective covering. It acts as the initial point of contact with customers and has a big influence on their choice of products. Packaging that is visually appealing and innovative tells the brand story in addition to improving product visibility on shelves. Packaging that is eco-friendly and sustainable supports the growing consumer awareness of environmental responsibility and enhances brand perception.

CHANNELS OF DISTRIBUTION

Any company looking to develop sustainably must start with creating a marketing plan. This thorough road map describes the objectives, target market, financial allotment, and methods for connecting with and interacting with clients. A carefully thought-out marketing strategy considers competitive analysis, market research, and a distinct grasp of the USP. It gives marketing initiatives a disciplined strategy that helps companies flourish in ever-changing market environments.

Distribution channels are essential for getting goods from producers to customers. The distribution channels used are determined by several variables, including the product's characteristics, the target market, and the company's goals. While indirect distribution may involve middlemen like wholesalers, distributors, or retailers, direct distribution entails selling goods directly to customers. To ensure that products are easily accessible to the intended audience and for supply chain management to be effective, it is imperative to strike an appropriate balance between various channels.

E-COMMERCE AND INTERNET MARKETING

Particularly in the digital age, online marketing, and e-commerce are becoming essential parts of contemporary marketing strategy. Businesses may reach a worldwide audience and establish direct connections with customers through the Internet. Email marketing, content marketing, search engine optimization (SEO), social media marketing, and other strategies are all included in online marketing. Conversely, e-commerce makes it easier for people to buy and sell goods and services online, giving customers convenience and accessibility while giving businesses access to new sources of income.

A comprehensive approach incorporating branding, packaging, a well-planned marketing strategy, a thoughtful selection of distribution channels, a strong web presence, and e-commerce capabilities is necessary for an effective marketing strategy. Together, these factors produce a unified and powerful marketing ecosystem that not only draws in clients but also forges enduring bonds with them, supporting the expansion and success of brands.

CHAPTER EIGHT

BUDGETING AND FINANCIAL MANAGEMENT FOR MELON FARMING

A key component of financial management in melon farming is budgeting, which entails organizing and assigning funds for a range of tasks related to melon cultivation. Farmers may more accurately project the expenditures associated with each phase of melon production—seed procurement, land preparation, irrigation, fertilization, pest control, and harvesting—by using a well-structured budget. It functions as a financial planning road map, empowering farmers to decide on resource allocation and possible returns on investment with knowledge.

ANALYZING COSTS

An integral part of melon farming's financial management is cost analysis. It entails a thorough analysis and breakdown of every cost related to the production process.

This covers permanent expenditures like labor, equipment, and land leases in addition to variable costs like insecticides, fertilizers, and seeds. Farmers can enhance the profitability and sustainability of their melon farming endeavor by implementing cost-saving measures or efficiency improvements in areas that they can identify via studying the cost structure.

STRATEGIES FOR PRICING

The financial viability of melon farming enterprises is significantly dependent on pricing tactics. Farmers must take into account several variables, including consumer perception of value, rival pricing, market demand, and production costs. It's critical to strike a balance between guaranteeing profitability and providing competitive prices.

Additionally, melon growers can improve their financial resilience and manage unpredictable economic settings by implementing variable pricing techniques that consider market conditions.

KEEPING UP WITH FINANCIAL DOCUMENTS

Maintaining accurate financial records is essential to successful financial management in the melon farming industry. Farmers may manage revenue and expenses, keep an eye on cash flow, and evaluate the operation's overall financial health with the help of accurate and thorough record-keeping.

Making educated decisions, obtaining loans or investments, and adhering to regulations all benefit greatly from this information. By streamlining the record-keeping process and enabling proactive financial management, current accounting tools and technologies may give farmers instantaneous insights into their financial performance.

Careful cost analysis, strategic budgeting, deliberate pricing tactics, and precise financial record-keeping are all necessary for effective financial management in melon farming.

Melon growers may maximize resource allocation, increase profitability, and guarantee the long-term sustainability of their agricultural ventures by incorporating these ideas into their farming techniques.

CHAPTER NINE

REGULATORY AND LEGAL ASPECTS

PERMITS AND LICENSES

Permits and licensing are essential to the business environment because they allow businesses to function within the law. To guarantee compliance with regulatory standards, getting the required licenses and permissions is crucial in several industries, including agriculture.

Within the agricultural industry, these permissions could cover, among other things, pesticide use, water rights, land use, and animal husbandry.

Businesses have a responsibility to fully comprehend and abide by the particular licensing requirements that are relevant to their operations, as failing to do so may result in penalties, fines, or even the suspension of operations.

OBSERVANCE OF AGRICULTURAL REGULATIONS

Adherence to regulatory requirements is crucial in the agriculture sector to guarantee the security and excellence of agricultural output. These regulations are set and enforced by governments and regulatory agencies to protect the environment, preserve ethical farming methods, and protect public health. Regulations about agriculture frequently address topics like food safety, animal welfare, and the use of fertilizers and pesticides.

Enterprises functioning in the agricultural domain ought to allocate resources toward a thorough comprehension and execution of these guidelines to minimize hazards and cultivate a favorable image within the sector.

SUSTAINABILITY AND ITS EFFECT ON THE ENVIRONMENT

Sustainability and its influence on the environment are now key factors in contemporary farming methods. Agricultural firms are under more pressure to reduce their environmental impact as the whole community recognizes the need for sustainable development.

As part of initiatives to improve agricultural sustainability, techniques including organic farming, water management, and soil conservation are becoming more and more popular. Following environmental laws is not just required by law but also morally right because it helps to maintain ecosystems and biodiversity. Therefore, to comply with changing legal requirements and social norms, agricultural businesses are urged to use environmentally conscious strategies, such as resource efficiency and pollution reduction.

The legal and regulatory environment for enterprises in the agriculture sector is shaped by the interconnected aspects of licensing and permits, adherence to agricultural rules, and environmental effects and sustainability. Following these principles is crucial for preserving legal standing as well as for the general welfare of ecosystems, communities, and the industry at large. Companies that put these factors first show that they are dedicated to moral and ethical behavior, setting themselves up for long-term success in a constantly changing regulatory landscape.

www.ingramcontent.com/pod-product-compliance
Lightning Source LLC
Chambersburg PA
CBHW070837290526
45795CB00002B/898